NUTRI NINJA

COMPLETE
EXTRACTION SYSTEM™

75 Nutritious & Delicious RECIPES

Although every precaution has been taken in the preparation of this book, the publisher and authors assume no responsibility for errors or omissions. Nor is any liability assumed for damages resulting from the use of the information contained herein. Although every effort has been made to ensure that the information contained in this book is complete and accurate, neither the publisher nor the authors are engaged in rendering professional advice or services to the individual reader. This information is not intended to replace the advice of a medical practitioner and consumers should always consult with a health care professional prior to making changes to diet or lifestyle, including any new health-related eating programs. Neither the publisher nor author shall be held responsible for any loss or damage allegedly arising from any information or suggestion in this book. The opinions expressed in this book represent the personal views of the authors and not that of the publisher.

Nutritional Analyses: Calculations for the nutritional analyses in this book are based on the largest number of servings listed within the recipes. Calculations are rounded up to the nearest gram or milligram, as appropriate. If two options for an ingredient are listed, the first one is used. Not included are optional ingredients or serving suggestions.

Editors and Content: Donna Scocozza, Culinary Director, Katie Barry, Lauren Nelson, Reggie Macon

Recipe Development: Euro-Pro® Culinary Innovation Team and Great Flavors Recipe Development Team

Graphic Designer: Leslie Anne Feagley

Creative/Photo Director: Keith Manning

Photography: Quentin Bacon and Gary Sloan

Published in the United States of America by

Great Flavors, LLC
P.O. Box 150
New Hope, PA 18938

ISBN: 978-1-4951-3387-9

10   9   8   7   6   5   4   3   2   1

Printed in China

Table of Contents

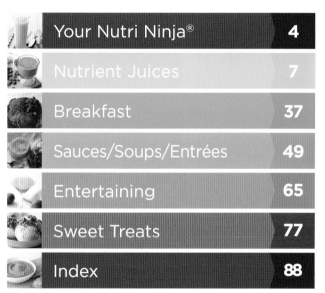
Follow us online for additional recipes and tips.

Your Nutri Ninja® Complete Extraction System™

Congratulations on starting your journey toward optimal wellness with your new Nutri Ninja®!

Now, you can easily blend vegetables, fruits, herbs, nuts, seeds, and other nutrient-packed ingredients to create nutrient-complete juices, sauces, soups, dips, and healthier desserts.

Kale and Sunflower Pesto page 51

The combination of the powerful motor and patented blade system work together to create smooth textures. Plus, this innovative combo can handle hard ingredients, such as ice, kale, fibrous greens, pulpy fruits, flax seeds, and nuts. The end result? Delicious nutritional goodness!

New to this? We've got you covered. Choose from our delicious recipes. Plus, we have helpful tips to customize your own! Our recipes include:

- high-nutrient, low-starch vegetables
- low sugar fruits
- detoxifying herbs
- super-food ingredients

Notes and helpful tips from our registered dietitians and nutritionists teach you about the basics of nutrient extract juicing. How much easier could it be—your daily dose of vegetables and fruits is just a few sips away.

Check out **NinjaKitchen.com/recipes**
for additional recipes and tips!

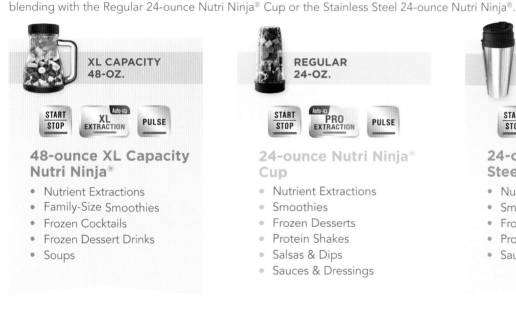

The Nutri Ninja® Complete Extraction System™ has accessories that are specially designed to perform unique functions. We have provided some recommendations for each accessory. For perfect pulsing, we recommend using **long pulses,** in 1 second lengths, to chop ingredients when blending with the XL Capacity 48-ounce Nutri Ninja®. Use **short pulses,** in half second lengths, to chop ingredients when blending with the Regular 24-ounce Nutri Ninja® Cup or the Stainless Steel 24-ounce Nutri Ninja®.

XL CAPACITY 48-OZ.

START STOP | XL EXTRACTION | PULSE

48-ounce XL Capacity Nutri Ninja®

- Nutrient Extractions
- Family-Size Smoothies
- Frozen Cocktails
- Frozen Dessert Drinks
- Soups

REGULAR 24-OZ.

START STOP | PRO EXTRACTION | PULSE

24-ounce Nutri Ninja® Cup

- Nutrient Extractions
- Smoothies
- Frozen Desserts
- Protein Shakes
- Salsas & Dips
- Sauces & Dressings

STAINLESS STEEL 24-OZ.

START STOP | PRO EXTRACTION | PULSE

24-ounce Stainless Steel Nutri Ninja®

- Nutrient Extractions
- Smoothies
- Frozen Treats
- Protein Shakes
- Sauces & Dips

NOTE: DO NOT BLEND HOT FOODS OR HOT LIQUIDS IN ANY NUTRI NINJA CUP OR JAR.

Why Nutrient Extract?

Nutrient extracted juices provide you with a simple way to boost your daily recommended nutritional intake. Key benefits include:

- Slower absorption of nutrients vs. juicing—more continual energy source
- Good source of nutrition—easy way to get your daily servings of fruits and vegetables
- Great variety of ingredients, textures, and flavor options
- Can be a quick and easy meal replacement
- Easy additions of protein and "good fats"
- Unlike juicing, adds fiber to your diet

Check out **NinjaKitchen.com/recipes** for additional Health Tips!

Lean Green Ninja
page 16

Kicked-Up Veggie Juice
page 23

Nutrient Juices

Power Ball

Start your day off right with this luscious energy booster. Fresh or frozen, blueberries are full of antioxidants and phytonutrients.

Ingredients

1 small ripe banana

¾ cup unsweetened light coconut milk

½ teaspoon unsweetened cocoa powder

¾ cup frozen blueberries

Directions

1 Place all ingredients into the Regular 24-ounce Nutri Ninja® Cup or the Stainless Steel Nutri Ninja® in the order listed.

2 Select Auto-iQ™ PRO EXTRACTION.

NUTRITIONALS (PER SERVING): CALORIES 260; FAT 10G; SODIUM 60MG; CARBOHYDRATES 45G; SUGAR 26G; FIBER 7G; PROTEIN 2G

NINJA KNOW-HOW   ADD 1 TABLESPOON MACA POWDER FOR A SUPER FOOD BOOST.

Green Light

The bright tropical flavors of this smoothie will keep you going all day.

Ingredients

½ medium cucumber, peeled, cut in 1-inch chunks

¾ cup fresh pineapple chunks

¾ cup frozen mango chunks

1 cup coconut water

Directions

1 Place all ingredients into the Regular 24-ounce Nutri Ninja® Cup or the Stainless Steel Nutri Ninja® in the order listed.

2 Select Auto-iQ™ PRO EXTRACTION.

NUTRITIONALS (PER SERVING): CALORIES 90; FAT .5G; SODIUM 130MG; CARBOHYDRATES 22G; SUGAR 17G; FIBER 3G; PROTEIN 2G

PREP TIME: 5 minutes   SERVINGS: 2   CONTAINER: Regular 24-ounce Nutri Ninja® Cup/ Stainless Steel Nutri Ninja®

Super Green Smoothie

This tasty green smoothie is the perfect between-meal refresher.

Ingredients

3-inch piece peeled English cucumber, cut in 1-inch chunks

½ cup packed baby spinach

12 green grapes

⅓ cup honeydew melon chunks

½ orange, peeled

½ cup ice

½ cup water

Directions

1 Place all ingredients into the Regular 24-ounce Nutri Ninja® Cup or the Stainless Steel Nutri Ninja® in the order listed.

2 Select Auto-iQ™ PRO EXTRACTION.

NUTRITIONALS (PER SERVING): CALORIES 80; FAT 0G; SODIUM 30MG; CARBOHYDRATES 19G; SUGAR 16G; FIBER 2G; PROTEIN 1G

Sweet Spinach Detox

Need more iron and spinach in your diet? This delicious citrus & green concoction will help your body absorb iron more easily.

Ingredients

½ cup fresh pineapple chunks

½-inch piece peeled fresh ginger

1 apple, cut into eight pieces

¼ medium lemon, peeled and seeded

1 tablespoon agave nectar or honey

½ cup apple juice

½ cup water

½ cup ice

Directions

1 Place all ingredients into the Regular 24-ounce Nutri Ninja® Cup or the Stainless Steel Nutri Ninja® in the order listed.

2 Select Auto-iQ™ PRO EXTRACTION.

NUTRITIONALS (PER SERVING): CALORIES 90; FAT 0G; SODIUM 15MG; CARBOHYDRATES 23G; SUGAR 18G; FIBER 3G; PROTEIN 1G

Check out **NinjaKitchen.com/recipes** for additional recipes and tips!

PREP TIME: 5 minutes   SERVINGS: 2   CONTAINER: Regular 24-ounce Nutri Ninja® Cup/Stainless Steel Nutri Ninja®

Carrot Tip Top

This is a powerhouse of vitamin A, great for vision and glowing skin!

Ingredients

2 medium carrots, peeled and cut into 1-inch pieces

1 cup carrot juice

2 tablespoons flax seeds

½ cup silken tofu

1 cup ice

Directions

1 Place all ingredients into the Regular 24-ounce Nutri Ninja® Cup or the Stainless Steel Nutri Ninja® in the order listed.

2 Select Auto-iQ™ PRO EXTRACTION.

NUTRITIONALS (PER SERVING): CALORIES 150; FAT 5G; SODIUM 140MG; CARBOHYDRATES 22G; SUGAR 9G; FIBER 5G; PROTEIN 6G

Frozen Kale Cacao

Known as the "queen of greens", kale is recognized for its exceptional nutrient richness, and many health benefits.

Ingredients

1 tablespoon unsweetened cocoa powder

3 pitted dates

1 small frozen banana, cut in half

¾ cup packed kale

1 cup unsweetened light coconut milk

½ cup ice

Directions

1 Place all ingredients into the Regular 24-ounce Nutri Ninja® Cup or the Stainless Steel Nutri Ninja® in the order listed.

2 Select Auto-iQ™ PRO EXTRACTION.

NUTRITIONALS (PER SERVING): CALORIES 240; FAT 7G; SODIUM 40MG; CARBOHYDRATES 48G; SUGAR 26G; FIBER 7G; PROTEIN 6G

ADD 2 TABLESPOONS CACAO NIBS FOR A SUPER FOOD BOOST, WITH THE BENEFITS OF DARK CHOCOLATE WITHOUT SUGAR.

PREP TIME: 5 minutes   SERVINGS: 2   CONTAINER: Regular 24-ounce Nutri Ninja® Cup/ Stainless Steel Nutri Ninja®

Berry Healthy Smoothie

Spinach blends perfectly with the flavor and natural sweetness of fruit.

Ingredients

½ cup ice

½ cup packed baby spinach

½ cup water

½ cup hulled fresh strawberries

½ cup blueberries

1 cup fresh mango chunks

½ cup fresh pineapple chunks

Directions

1 Place all ingredients into the Regular 24-ounce Nutri Ninja® Cup or the Stainless Steel Nutri Ninja® in the order listed.

2 Select Auto-iQ™ PRO EXTRACTION.

NUTRITIONALS (PER SERVING): CALORIES 110; FAT .5G; SODIUM 10MG; CARBOHYDRATES 28G; SUGAR 22G; FIBER 3G; PROTEIN 2G;

Spicy Pineapple Recharge

Sweet and spicy defines this refreshing drink. Try it as an afternoon snack.

Ingredients

½ small jalapeño pepper, seeded

½-inch piece peeled fresh ginger

1 lime, peeled and cut in half

2 cups fresh pineapple chunks

⅔ cup orange juice

½ cup ice

Directions

1 Place all ingredients into the Regular 24-ounce Nutri Ninja® Cup or the Stainless Steel Nutri Ninja® in the order listed.

2 Select Auto-iQ™ PRO EXTRACTION.

NUTRITIONALS (PER SERVING): CALORIES 130; FAT 0G; SODIUM 5MG; CARBOHYDRATES 33G; SUGAR 16G; FIBER 3G; PROTEIN 2G

Lean Green Ninja

Our favorite green smoothie is perfect for the whole family. The sweet flavors of pineapple and mango will wake up the tastebuds.

Ingredients

1 small ripe banana

½ cup packed kale leaves

½ cup packed baby spinach

1 cup fresh pineapple chunks

1 cup fresh mango chunks

1 cup ice

1 cup coconut water

Directions

1 Place all ingredients into the XL Capacity 48-ounce Nutri Ninja® in the order listed.

2 Select Auto-iQ™ XL EXTRACTION.

NUTRITIONALS (PER SERVING): CALORIES 78; FAT 1G; CHOLESTEROL 0MG; SODIUM 11MG; CARBOHYDRATES 20G; FIBER 3G; PROTEIN 4G

Broc & Roll

Research has shown that just 2 tablespoons of broccoli sprouts contain as much detoxifying glucoraphanin as 2 pounds of fully mature broccoli.

Ingredients

2 tablespoons broccoli sprouts

½ lime, peeled

¼ cup chopped celery

¼ ripe avocado, pitted and peeled

1 cup water

½ cup frozen raspberries

Directions

1 Place all ingredients into the Regular 24-ounce Nutri Ninja® Cup or the Stainless Steel Nutri Ninja® in the order listed.

2 Select Auto-iQ™ PRO EXTRACTION.

NUTRITIONALS (PER SERVING): CALORIES 130; FAT 8G; SODIUM 45MG; CARBOHYDRATES 17G; SUGAR 4G; FIBER 8G; PROTEIN 3G

17

Veggie Power

Quick and easy, this veggie delight is an awesome way to get a boost of vitamin C and iron.

Ingredients

½ vine-ripe tomato, cut into 2 pieces

½ cup packed baby spinach

2 celery stalks, each cut into 4 pieces

½ cup broccoli florets

4 fresh basil leaves

¼ unpeeled uncored apple

½ teaspoon ground black pepper

1¾ cups water

¾ cup ice

Directions

1 Place all ingredients into the XL Capacity 48-ounce Nutri Ninja® in the order listed.

2 Select Auto-iQ™ XL EXTRACTION.

NUTRITIONALS (PER SERVING): CALORIES 30; FAT 0G; SODIUM 60MG; CARBOHYDRATES 6G; SUGAR 4G; FIBER 2G; PROTEIN 2G

NINJA KNOW-HOW FOR A FLAVOR BOOST, ADD ⅛ TEASPOON GARLIC POWDER AFTER THE BLACK PEPPER

Cherry-Limeade

This refreshing homemade sports drink will remind you of a childhood favorite!

Ingredients

1¼ cups frozen pitted cherries

2 tablespoons lime juice

2½ cups coconut water

Directions

1 Place all ingredients into the XL Capacity 48-ounce Nutri Ninja® in the order listed.

2 Select Auto-iQ™ XL EXTRACTION.

3 Pour mixture through a fine mesh strainer to extract the flavored water.

4 Store in refrigerator for up to 3 days.

NUTRITIONALS (PER SERVING): CALORIES 100; FAT 1G; SODIUM 280MG; CARBOHYDRATES 24G; SUGAR 18G; FIBER 4G; PROTEIN 4G

NINJA KNOW-HOW   STIR IN 2 TABLESPOONS WHITE CHIA SEEDS FOR A HOMEMADE CHIA FRESCA FULL OF PROTEIN!

PREP TIME: 5 minutes   SERVINGS: 2   CONTAINER: Regular 24-ounce Nutri Ninja® Cup/ Stainless Steel Nutri Ninja®

Purple Potion

Beets contain many of the necessary vitamins and micronutrients that support the production and maintenance of our bodies' cells.

Ingredients

¾ cup roasted beet chunks

1¼ cups carrot juice

1 cup frozen blueberries

Directions

1 Place all ingredients into the Regular 24-ounce Nutri Ninja® Cup or the Stainless Steel Nutri Ninja® in the order listed.

2 Select Auto-iQ™ PRO EXTRACTION.

NUTRITIONALS (PER SERVING): CALORIES 130; FAT 1G; SODIUM 150MG; CARBOHYDRATES 30G; SUGAR 17G; FIBER 5G; PROTEIN 3G

 NINJA® KNOW-HOW   ADD 2 TEASPOONS AÇAI POWDER FOR A SUPER FOOD BOOST.

PREP TIME: 5 minutes   SERVINGS: 1   CONTAINER: Regular 24-ounce Nutri Ninja® Cup/Stainless Steel Nutri Ninja®

Pear Cleanse

Bok choy plus cilantro can help your body's detoxifying process.

Ingredients

¾ cup chopped bok choy

¼ cup fresh cilantro

1 ripe pear, cored, cut in quarters

⅛ ripe avocado, pitted and peeled

1 teaspoon lime juice

½ pitted date

½ cup chilled brewed holy basil or tulsi tea

¼ cup ice

Directions

1 Place all ingredients into the Regular 24-ounce Nutri Ninja® Cup or the Stainless Steel Nutri Ninja® in the order listed.

2 Select Auto-iQ™ PRO EXTRACTION.

NUTRITIONALS (PER SERVING): CALORIES 160; FAT 4G; SODIUM 40MG; CARBOHYDRATES 34G; SUGAR 21G; FIBER 8G; PROTEIN 2G

NINJA KNOW-HOW ADD ½ TEASPOON FLAX SEED OIL TO ROUND OUT THE FLAVORS, BRINGING A NUTTY QUALITY WITH ADDED NUTRITION.

PREP TIME: 5 minutes   SERVINGS: 1   CONTAINER: Regular 24-ounce Nutri Ninja® Cup/Stainless Steel Nutri Ninja®

Chai-Spiced Eye Opener

Kick-start your morning with a refreshing combination of fruit, greens, and spiced tea. Your taste buds will thank you!

Ingredients

1 ripe pear, quartered and cored

1 cup loosely packed baby spinach

1 cup chilled, brewed chai tea (from tea bag)

¼-inch piece peeled fresh ginger

½ cup frozen mango chunks

2 teaspoons fresh lemon juice

Dash sea salt

Directions

1 Place all ingredients into the Regular 24-ounce Nutri Ninja® Cup or the Stainless Steel Nutri Ninja® in the order listed.

2 Select Auto-iQ™ PRO EXTRACTION.

NUTRITIONALS (PER SERVING): CALORIES 160; FAT .5G; SODIUM 320MG; CARBOHYDRATES 41G; SUGAR 29G; FIBER 8G; PROTEIN 2G

Kicked-Up Veggie Juice

Combining eight vitamin-packed vegetables with apples produce a vitamin A, B, and C-rich super juice loaded with fiber.

Ingredients

3-inch piece English cucumber, cut into 4 pieces

¼ small green apple, cut into 2 pieces

1 small carrot, peeled and cut into 2 pieces

⅛ small red onion

¼ jalapeño pepper, seeded

¼ small beet, peeled

¼ cup coarsely chopped red cabbage

½ cup ice

1 small vine-ripe tomato, cut into 4 pieces

¼ teaspoon sea salt

Directions

1 Place all ingredients into the Regular 24-ounce Nutri Ninja® Cup or the Stainless Steel Nutri Ninja® in the order listed.

2 Select Auto-iQ™ PRO EXTRACTION.

NUTRITIONALS (PER SERVING): CALORIES 40; FAT 0G; SODIUM 320MG; CARBOHYDRATES 9G; SUGAR 6G; FIBER 2G; PROTEIN 1G

NUTRIENT JUICES

Strawberry-Melon Energy Blast

Perfect refresher packed with your vitamin C for the day!

Ingredients

8-inch piece peeled English cucumber, cut into 2-inch chunks

1¾ cups cantaloupe chunks

10 hulled fresh strawberries

½ cup ice

1 cup water

Directions

1 Place all ingredients into the XL Capacity 48-ounce Nutri Ninja® in the order listed.

2 Select Auto-iQ™ XL EXTRACTION.

NUTRITIONALS (PER SERVING):CALORIES 70; FAT .5G; SODIUM 25MG; CARBOHYDRATES 17G; SUGAR 15G; FIBER 3G; PROTEIN 2G

Pineapple-Mint Water

Keep this drink on hand in the fridge for a sweet and soothing treat for the entire family!

Ingredients

¾ cup fresh pineapple chunks

4 fresh mint leaves

4½ cups water

Directions

1 Place all ingredients into the XL Capacity 48-ounce Nutri Ninja® in the order listed.

2 Select Auto-iQ™ XL EXTRACTION.

3 Pour mixture through a fine mesh strainer to extract the flavored water.

4 Store in refrigerator for up to 3 days.

NUTRITIONALS (PER SERVING): CALORIES 15; FAT 0G; SODIUM 10MG;
CARBOHYDRATES 4G; SUGAR 3G; FIBER 0G; PROTEIN 0G

Kiwi Cooler

Who knew green could be so yummy? A perfect super juice filled with antioxidants!

Ingredients

2 pitted dates

1 medium stalk celery, cut into
   4 pieces

1 ripe kiwi, peeled and cut in half

1 cup chopped cabbage

1 cup loosely packed kale leaves

1⅓ cups hazelnut milk

1 cup ice

Directions

1 Soak the dates in 1 cup of warm water for 30 minutes; drain and set aside.

2 Place the dates and all remaining ingredients into the Regular 24-ounce Nutri Ninja® Cup or the Stainless Steel Nutri Ninja® in the order listed.

3 Select Auto-iQ™ PRO EXTRACTION.

NUTRITIONALS (PER SERVING): CALORIES 150; FAT 3G; SODIUM 115MG; CARBOHYDRATES 29G; SUGAR 17G; FIBER 4G; PROTEIN 5G

Watermelon Cooler

Just three ingredients make this a super-easy and super-refreshing anytime drink.

Ingredients

¼ pear, seeded, cut in half

2 large fresh basil leaves

2 cups chilled watermelon chunks

Directions

1 Place all ingredients into the Regular 24-ounce Nutri Ninja® Cup or the Stainless Steel Nutri Ninja® in the order listed.

2 Select Auto-iQ™ PRO EXTRACTION.

NUTRITIONALS (PER SERVING): CALORIES 60; FAT 0G; SODIUM 0MG; CARBOHYDRATES 15G; SUGAR 12G; FIBER 1G; PROTEIN 1G

NUTRIENT JUICES

Ginger Greens

Considered two of the ultimate "detox" foods, kale and cilantro combine to cleanse your system! The avocado lends a rich, creamy consistency and a dose of "good" monounsaturated fat.

Ingredients

¾ cup packed baby kale

¼ cup fresh cilantro

¼ ripe avocado, pitted and peeled

1 pitted date

2 ripe kiwis, each peeled and quartered

1 teaspoon lime juice

½-inch piece peeled fresh ginger

¼ cup coconut water

¼ cup ice

Directions

1 Place all ingredients into the Regular 24-ounce Nutri Ninja® Cup or the Stainless Steel Nutri Ninja® in the order listed.

2 Select Auto-iQ™ PRO EXTRACTION.

NUTRITIONALS (PER SERVING): CALORIES 220; FAT 9G; SODIUM 95MG; CARBOHYDRATES 37G; SUGAR 19G; FIBER 10G; PROTEIN 5G;

 NINJA KNOW-HOW **FOR AN EXTRA DETOXIFYING BONUS, ADD ½ TEASPOON CHLORELLA POWDER.**

PREP TIME: 5 minutes   SERVINGS: 2   CONTAINER: Regular 24-ounce Nutri Ninja® Cup/Stainless Steel Nutri Ninja®

Gold & Green

Share this re-hydrating smoothie with your workout buddy!

Ingredients

½ medium golden delicious apple, cored and cut into 4 pieces

½ cup loosely packed baby spinach

¼ cup green seedless grapes

1 teaspoon lime juice

½ cup ice

½ cup coconut water

Directions

1 Place all ingredients into the Regular 24-ounce Nutri Ninja® Cup or the Stainless Steel Nutri Ninja® in the order listed.

2 Select Auto-iQ™ PRO EXTRACTION.

NUTRITIONALS (PER SERVING): CALORIES 45; FAT 0G; SODIUM 70MG; CARBOHYDRATES 11G; SUGAR 8G; FIBER 2G; PROTEIN <1G

NUTRIENT JUICES

Pineapple Pleaser

This pineapple-papaya combo is full-flavored and high in vitamin C.

Ingredients

¾ cup fresh ripe papaya chunks

1¼ cups original rice milk

1 tablespoon cashew butter

1 cup frozen pineapple chunks

Directions

1 Place all ingredients into the Regular 24-ounce Nutri Ninja® Cup or the Stainless Steel Nutri Ninja® in the order listed.

2 Select Auto-iQ™ PRO EXTRACTION.

NUTRITIONALS (PER SERVING): CALORIES 190; FAT 5G; SODIUM 95MG; CARBOHYDRATES 35G; SUGAR 20G; FIBER 2G; PROTEIN 3G

Ginger-Pear Defense

Ginger is a natural anti-inflammatory and a known stomach soother.

Ingredients

1 ripe pear, cored

½ cup cantaloupe chunks

¼ lemon peeled, seeded

½-inch piece peeled fresh ginger

½ cup ice

Directions

1 Place all ingredients into the Regular 24-ounce Nutri Ninja® Cup or the Stainless Steel Nutri Ninja® in the order listed.

2 Select Auto-iQ™ PRO EXTRACTION.

NUTRITIONALS (PER SERVING): CALORIES 45; FAT 0G; SODIUM 10MG; CARBOHYDRATES 11G; SUGAR 9G; FIBER 0G; PROTEIN 0G

 NINJA KNOW-HOW   ADD 1 TABLESPOON BEE POLLEN FOR A SUPER FOOD BOOST.

NUTRIENT JUICES

PREP TIME: 5 minutes SERVINGS: 2 CONTAINER: Regular 24-ounce Nutri Ninja® Cup/Stainless Steel Nutri Ninja®

Gingered Açai

Açai and pomegranate, prized for having antioxidants, plus ginger, an anti-inflammatory and great for digestion, make the perfect combination beverage for your busy day!

Ingredients

½ cup unsweetened açai berry purée, thawed

1 packet (.035 ounce) stevia

½-inch piece peeled fresh ginger

1½ cups pomegranate juice

1½ cups frozen strawberries

Directions

1 Place all ingredients into the Regular 24-ounce Nutri Ninja® Cup or the Stainless Steel Nutri Ninja® in the order listed.

2 Select Auto-iQ™ PRO EXTRACTION.

NUTRITIONALS (PER SERVING): CALORIES 100; FAT 2G; SODIUM 10MG; CARBOHYDRATES 20G; SUGAR 16G; FIBER 2G; PROTEIN <1G

 SUBSTITUTE MIXED BERRIES OR RASPBERRIES FOR A TASTY ALTERNATIVE.

Watermelon Quencher

Drink in the flavor of summer all year long with this wonderfully refreshing thirst quencher that's loaded with phytonutrients!

Ingredients

2½ cups watermelon chunks

2 cups pomegranate juice

1 cup frozen peach slices

Directions

1 Place all ingredients into the XL Capacity 48-ounce Nutri Ninja® in the order listed.

2 Select Auto-iQ™ XL EXTRACTION.

NUTRITIONALS (PER SERVING): CALORIES 150; FAT .5G; SODIUM 15MG;
CARBOHYDRATES 39G; SUGAR 36G; FIBER 2G; PROTEIN 1G

PREP TIME: 5 minutes   MAKES: 4½ cups   CONTAINER: XL Capacity 48-ounce Nutri Ninja®

Almond Milk

Almond milk is lower in calories than cow's milk, and it's also lactose free. Keep it on hand to enjoy in any smoothie.

Ingredients

1½ cups raw almonds

4½ cups water

⅛ teaspoon sea salt

Directions

1 Place all ingredients into the XL Capacity 48-ounce Nutri Ninja® in the order listed.

2 Select Auto-iQ™ XL EXTRACTION.

3 Pour mixture through a filtration bag or a fine mesh strainer to extract milk.

4 Store extracted milk in refrigerator for up to 3 days.

NUTRITIONALS (PER 1/2 CUP SERVING): CALORIES 30; FAT 1.5G; SODIUM 105MG; CARBOHYDRATES 4G; SUGAR 3G; FIBER 0G; PROTEIN 1G

EXPERIMENT WITH OTHER MILKS— CASHEWS, HAZELNUTS, OATS, AND HEMP SEEDS WORK GREAT.

Island Mood Boost

Everyone's mood is bound to improve while sipping this yummy tropical fruit smoothie. Serve it as an after-school snack or afternoon pick me up.

Ingredients

2 cups coconut water

1 cup fresh pineapple chunks

1 small ripe banana

1 cup frozen mango chunks

1 cup frozen strawberries

Directions

1 Place all ingredients into the XL Capacity 48-ounce Nutri Ninja® in the order listed.

2 Select Auto-iQ™ XL EXTRACTION.

NUTRITIONALS (PER SERVING): CALORIES 100; FAT .5G; SODIUM 130MG; CARBOHYDRATES 24G; SUGAR 17G; FIBER 4G; PROTEIN 1G

Spiced Cucumber Cooler

Cool, refreshing, and only 50 calories, this drink is a perfect rehydrator after exercising.

Ingredients

4-inch piece English cucumber, cut into 1-inch chunks

½ cup cantaloupe chunks

½ jalapeño pepper, seeded

½ cup green seedless grapes

1 cup water

½ cup ice

Directions

1 Place all ingredients into the Regular 24-ounce Nutri Ninja® Cup or the Stainless Steel Nutri Ninja® in the order listed.

2 Select Auto-iQ™ PRO EXTRACTION.

NUTRITIONALS (PER SERVING): CALORIES 50; FAT 0G; SODIUM 15MG; CARBOHYDRATES 13G; SUGAR 10G; FIBER 1G; PROTEIN 1G

NINJA KNOW-HOW   CUCUMBERS ARE A GREAT SOURCE OF B VITAMINS AND CARBOHYDRATES.

Coffee Soymoothie
page 42

PREP TIME: 10 minutes + 3 minutes cook   **SERVINGS: 4**   CONTAINER: Regular 24-ounce Nutri Ninja® Cup/Stainless Steel Nutri Ninja®

Tomato-Basil Scramble

This recipe is an easy and simple way to make fluffy eggs and veggies in the morning!

Ingredients

8 large eggs

½ cup chopped seeded vine-ripe tomato

½ cup shredded mozzarella cheese

½ cup loosely packed fresh basil leaves

¼ teaspoon salt

¼ teaspoon ground black pepper

4 teaspoons unsalted butter

Directions

1 Place the eggs, tomato, mozzarella, basil, salt, and black pepper into the Regular 24-ounce Nutri Ninja® Cup or the Stainless Steel Nutri Ninja®. PULSE 3 times, using short pulses, until chopped fine.

2 In a medium nonstick skillet, heat the butter over medium-high heat. Add the egg mixture, and cook, stirring frequently until fluffy and cooked through.

3 Divide between 4 plates.

NUTRITIONALS (PER SERVING): CALORIES 220; FAT 16G; SODIUM 350MG; CARBOHYDRATES 2G; SUGAR 1G; FIBER 0G; PROTEIN 17G

PREP TIME: 15 minutes + 30 minutes rest   BAKE TIME: 25 minutes   SERVINGS: 8   CONTAINER: Regular 24-ounce Nutri Ninja® Cup/Stainless Steel Nutri Ninja®

BREAKFAST

Spinach & Feta Strata

This classic egg-and-cheese casserole is as perfect for a light, weeknight supper as it is for a weekend brunch.

Ingredients

5 large eggs

1 cup half & half

½ cup cubed Monterey Jack cheese

½ cup cubed feta cheese

¼ teaspoon ground nutmeg

½ teaspoon salt

¼ teaspoon ground black pepper

1 cup frozen, thawed spinach, drained well

1 loaf day-old French bread, crusts removed, torn into bite-sized pieces

Directions

1 Lightly spray a 9-inch round baking pan with vegetable cooking spray; set aside. Add the eggs, half & half, Monterey Jack cheese, feta cheese, nutmeg, salt, and pepper to the Regular 24-ounce Nutri Ninja® Cup or the Stainless Steel Nutri Ninja®.

2 PULSE 5 times, using short pulses, then add the well-drained spinach. PULSE 2 times, using short pulses.

3 Place the bread into the pan and pour the spinach and egg mixture over the bread. Place into the refrigerator for 30 minutes to allow the egg mixture to soak into the bread.

4 Preheat oven to 350F°. Bake 20 to 25 minutes until cooked through and golden brown.

NUTRITIONALS (PER SERVING): CALORIES 310; FAT 12G; SODIUM 660MG; CARBOHYDRATES 35G; SUGAR 2G; FIBER 2G; PROTEIN 16G

BREAKFAST

Top O' The Mornin'

Start your day right with this simple, fresh and fiber-packed delight. Yum!

Ingredients

1 small ripe banana

1 orange, peeled, cut in half

1 cup unsweetened vanilla almond milk

½ teaspoon ground cinnamon

1 scoop whey protein powder

½ cup ice

Directions

1 Place all ingredients into the Regular 24-ounce Nutri Ninja® Cup or the Stainless Steel Nutri Ninja® in the order listed.

2 Select Auto-iQ™ PRO EXTRACTION.

NUTRITIONALS (PER SERVING): CALORIES 327; FAT 7G; SODIUM 223MG; CARBOHYDRATES 50G; SUGAR 25G; FIBER 10G; PROTEIN 21G

Trail Mix in a Glass

All the sweet and nutty flavors of trail mix, whipped up in a nourishing morning beverage. Go for it!

Ingredients

2 tablespoons raw almonds

2 tablespoons raw pumpkin seeds

2 teaspoons raw sesame seeds

2 tablespoons goji berries

2 tablespoons pomegranate juice concentrate

¾ cup unsweetened almond milk

2 tablespoons honey

½ cup ice

Directions

1 Place all ingredients into the Regular 24-ounce Nutri Ninja® Cup or the Stainless Steel Nutri Ninja® Cup in the order listed.

2 Select Auto-iQ™ PRO EXTRACTION.

NUTRITIONALS (PER SERVING): CALORIES 225; FAT 12G; SODIUM 100MG; CARBOHYDRATES 24G; SUGAR 18G; FIBER 3G; PROTEIN 7G

ADD 1 TABLESPOON BEE POLLEN FOR A SUPER FOOD BOOST.

BREAKFAST

Coffee Soymoothie

Packed with protein and rich coffee flavor, this creamy drink is sure to become a morning favorite.

Ingredients

1 cup cold strongly brewed coffee

⅔ cup silken tofu

4 teaspoons almond butter

¼ teaspoon ground cardamom

⅛ cup agave nectar

1 cup ice

Directions

1 Place all ingredients into the Regular 24-ounce Nutri Ninja® Cup or the Stainless Steel Nutri Ninja® in the order listed.

2 Select Auto-iQ™ PRO EXTRACTION.

NUTRITIONALS (PER SERVING): CALORIES 160; FAT 8G; SODIUM 30MG; CARBOHYDRATES 19G; SUGAR 17G; FIBER 1G; PROTEIN 6G

Almond Chai Tea

Chai tea, rich in antioxidants and spices, has been used for thousands of years to promote general health and well-being.

Ingredients

3 pitted dates

3 tablespoons raw almonds

½ small ripe banana

2 cups chilled strongly brewed Chai tea

Directions

1 Place all ingredients into the Regular 24-ounce Nutri Ninja® Cup or the Stainless Steel Nutri Ninja® in the order listed.

2 Select Auto-iQ™ PRO EXTRACTION.

NUTRITIONALS (PER SERVING): CALORIES 180; FAT 8G; SODIUM 0MG; CARBOHYDRATES 30G; SUGAR 25G; FIBER 4G; PROTEIN 4G

Banana & Oats

Here's a portable oatmeal breakfast loaded with micronutrient-rich walnuts and fruit. A great way to use any leftover oatmeal.

Ingredients

1 small ripe banana

1 tablespoon walnut pieces

1 cup nonfat milk

½ cup cold, cooked oatmeal

¼ teaspoon ground cinnamon

½ cup nonfat vanilla yogurt

Directions

1 Place all ingredients into the Regular 24-ounce Nutri Ninja® Cup or the Stainless Steel Nutri Ninja® in the order listed.

2 Select Auto-iQ™ PRO EXTRACTION.

NUTRITIONALS (PER SERVING): CALORIES 410; FAT 7G; SODIUM 180MG; CARBOHYDRATES 74G; SUGAR 45G; FIBER 5G; PROTEIN 18G

PREP TIME: 5 minutes   COOK TIME: 5 minutes   SERVINGS: 4   CONTAINER: Regular 24-ounce Nutri Ninja® Cup/Stainless Steel Nutri Ninja®

BREAKFAST

Buckwheat Boost Pancakes

Serve these flavorful pancakes topped with sliced fresh fruit like strawberries or peaches, and drizzled with honey.

Ingredients

1 cup low-fat buttermilk

1 egg

3 tablespoons canola oil

½ cup buckwheat flour

½ cup all-purpose flour

1 teaspoon baking soda

1 teaspoon sugar

½ teaspoon salt

1 tablespoon honey

Directions

1 Place the buttermilk, egg, and canola oil into the Regular 24-ounce Nutri Ninja® Cup or the Stainless Steel Nutri Ninja®.

2 Select START and blend for 5 seconds. Add the rest of the ingredients, and blend for an additional 5 seconds. Let batter sit for 1 hour.

3 On a lightly oiled skillet or griddle, over medium heat, pour pancake batter in desired size and cook until small bubbles form. Flip and continue cooking until center is puffed and springs back when gently pushed.

NUTRITIONALS (PER SERVING): CALORIES 290; FAT 12G; SODIUM 470MG; CARBOHYDRATES 40G; SUGAR 11G; FIBER 3G; PROTEIN 7G

Blueberry Super Crunch

Four super foods and the concentrated flavor of dried blueberries combine to make this a sure hit for breakfast or as a healthy snack.

Ingredients

½ cup raw almonds

1 tablespoon flax seeds

¼ cup dry-roasted pumpkin seeds

¼ cup hemp seeds

1 tablespoon chia seeds

½ teaspoon ground cinnamon

3 cups plain granola

½ cup dried blueberries

Directions

1 Place all ingredients, except for granola and blueberries, into the Stainless Steel Nutri Ninja® in the order listed.

2 PULSE 6 times, using long pulses.

3 In a medium mixing bowl, combine the ground mixture with the granola and blueberries.

4 Store in an airtight container until ready to use.

5 Enjoy with milk as cereal or atop your favorite low-fat yogurt.

NUTRITIONALS (PER SERVING): CALORIES 270; FAT 12G; SODIUM 15MG; CARBOHYDRATES 36G; SUGAR 13G; FIBER 5G; PROTEIN 7G;

Strawberry-Banana Smoothie

Some say this is the drink that started the smoothie craze! We just say it's delicious, and so will your family. Perfect for breakfast or all through the day.

BREAKFAST

Ingredients

2 small ripe bananas

2 cups low-fat milk

¼ cup agave nectar

2 cups frozen strawberries

Directions

1 Place all ingredients into the XL Capacity 48-ounce Nutri Ninja® in the order listed.

2 Select Auto-iQ™ XL EXTRACTION.

NUTRITIONALS (PER SERVING): CALORIES 240; FAT 3G; SODIUM 75MG; CARBOHYDRATES 53G; SUGAR 37G; FIBER 4G; PROTEIN 6G

Autumn Blush

Sweet potato, maple syrup, and turmeric combine in this flavorful fall favorite to make an afternoon or anytime pick-me-up.

Ingredients

- ¾ cup cold cooked sweet potato
- 1 cup unsweetened almond milk
- 2 tablespoons maple syrup
- 1 teaspoon flax seeds
- ¼ teaspoon ground turmeric
- ½ teaspoon salt
- ¾ cup ice

Directions

1 Place all ingredients into the Regular 24-ounce Nutri Ninja® Cup or the Stainless Steel Nutri Ninja® in the order listed.

2 Select Auto-iQ™ PRO EXTRACTION.

NUTRITIONALS (PER SERVING): CALORIES 130; FAT 2G; SODIUM 590MG; CARBOHYDRATES 28G; SUGAR 17G; FIBER 3G; PROTEIN 2G

Pineapple-Cilantro
Dipping Sauce
page 50

Pineapple-Cilantro Dipping Sauce

Of all the bright green herbs, cilantro—the fresh, antioxident-rich leafy stalks of the coriander plant— is loved by millions who us it in everything from soups and salsas, to wraps and roll-ups.

Ingredients

1 cup fresh pineapple chunks

1 small serrano chili pepper, seeded

½ small white onion, cut in 4 pieces

¼ cup fresh cilantro

2 tablespoons freshly squeezed lime juice

1 tablespoon coconut oil

¼ teaspoon salt

⅛ teaspoon ground black pepper

Directions

1 Place all ingredients into the Regular 24-ounce Nutri Ninja® Cup or the Stainless Steel Nutri Ninja® in the order listed.

2 PULSE 3 times, then select START and blend for 25 seconds.

NUTRITIONALS (PER ½ CUP SERVING): CALORIES 40; FAT 2.5G; SODIUM 0MG; CARBOHYDRATES 5G; SUGAR 3G; FIBER 1G; PROTEIN 0G

NINJA
KNOW-HOW
TO KEEP CILANTRO FRESH AND GREEN, WRAP IN A WET PAPER TOWEL AND STORE IN THE REFRIGERATOR CRISPER DRAWER.

PREP TIME: 25 minutes   COOK TIME: 30 seconds   MAKES: 1½ cups   CONTAINER: Regular 24-ounce Nutri Ninja® Cup/Stainless Steel Nutri Ninja®

Kale & Sunflower Pesto

A new twist on an old favorite! A great way to use up those extra greens—baby spinach works well, too!

Ingredients

¼ medium bunch kale, stems removed

¼ cup loosely packed fresh basil leaves

1 small clove garlic

2 tablespoons unsalted roasted sunflower seeds

1½-ounce chunk Parmesan cheese

Zest and juice of ½ lemon

¼ cup water

¼ teaspoon salt

¼ teaspoon ground black pepper

¼ cup olive oil plus more as needed

Directions

1 Bring 4 quarts of salted water to a boil. Blanch the kale for 30 seconds and, upon removal, immediately plunge into ice water. Squeeze the kale leaves dry and set aside.

2 Place the blanched kale and all remaining ingredients into the Regular 24-ounce Nutri Ninja® Cup or the Stainless Steel Nutri Ninja® in the order listed.

3 PULSE 3 times, using short pulses, then select START and blend for 15 seconds. Store in airtight container in the refrigerator up to 1 week or in the freezer up to 2 months.

NUTRITIONALS (PER ¼ CUP SERVING): CALORIES 120; FAT 12G; SODIUM 45MG; CARBOHYDRATES 3G; SUGAR 0G; FIBER 1G; PROTEIN 2G

PREP TIME: 5 minutes   COOK TIME: 25 minutes   MAKES: 2 cups   CONTAINER: Regular 24-ounce Nutri Ninja® Cup/Stainless Steel Nutri Ninja®

Sundried Tomato Sauce

Make homemade sauce with less sugar than what's found in store-bought sauces. Plus, this recipe is filled with lycopene!

Ingredients

½ tablespoon canola oil

½ yellow onion, chopped

2 cloves garlic, chopped

1 can (14 ounces) whole, peeled tomatoes and juice

3 ounces sundried tomatoes packed in olive oil

¼ cup dry red wine

¼ teaspoon red pepper flakes

¼ cup fresh basil leaves, loosely packed

salt and pepper to taste

Directions

1 Heat the oil in a 2-quart saucepan over medium heat. Add the onions and garlic then sauté for 5 minutes, until softened.

2 Place the tomatoes with juice, sun-dried tomatoes, red wine, and red pepper flakes into the Regular 24-ounce Nutri Ninja® Cup or the Stainless Steel Nutri Ninja® in the order listed.

3 PULSE 4 to 6 times, using long pulses, until desired consistency. For chunkier consistency, pulse only 4 times. Pulse longer for a smoother consistency.

4 Add the tomato purée to the saucepan with the garlic and onions. Simmer for 20 minutes. Add fresh basil just before removing from the heat. Serve immediately or store in the refrigerator up to 1 week.

NUTRITIONALS (PER 1/2 CUP SERVING): CALORIES 130; FAT 7G; SODIUM 150MG; CARBOHYDRATES 13G; SUGAR 6G; FIBER 2G; PROTEIN 2G

PREP TIME: 10 minutes   MAKES: 1¾ cups   CONTAINER: Regular 24-ounce Nutri Ninja® Cup/Stainless Steel Nutri Ninja®

Passion Fruit & Mustard Dressing

A smooth and creamy dressing that complements greens, fruit or chicken.

Ingredients

½ cup thawed frozen passion fruit pulp

2 tablespoons Dijon mustard

¼ cup rice wine vinegar

3 tablespoons honey

2 tablespoons fresh thyme leaves

½ teaspoon salt

3 tablespoons extra-virgin olive oil

¾ cup nonfat sour cream

Directions

1 Place all ingredients into the Regular 24-ounce Nutri Ninja® Cup or the Stainless Steel Nutri Ninja® in the order listed.

2 PULSE 3 times, using short pulses, then select START and blend for 25 seconds.

NUTRITIONALS (PER 2 TABLESPOON SERVING): CALORIES 30; FAT 3G; SODIUM 110MG; CARBOHYDRATES 8G; SUGAR 6G; FIBER 0G; PROTEIN 0G

 NINJA KNOW-HOW FOR A SWEET VARIATION, SUBSTITUTE REAL MAPLE SYRUP FOR THE HONEY.

Creamy Herb Dressing

Fresh herbs and ground black pepper are the secrets to a full-flavored dressing that will make you forget the bottled kind forever.

Ingredients

½ cup low-fat buttermilk

1 cup low-fat mayonnaise

1 tablespoon lemon juice

¼ cup fresh parsley leaves

12 sprigs fresh chives

⅓ cup tarragon leaves

1 clove garlic

1 teaspoon ground black pepper

½ teaspoon salt

Directions

1 Place all ingredients into the Regular 24-ounce Nutri Ninja® Cup or the Stainless Steel Nutri Ninja® in the order listed.

2 PULSE 3 times, using short pulses, then select START and blend for 25 seconds.

NUTRITIONALS (PER 2 TABLESPOON SERVING): CALORIES 70; FAT 7G; SODIUM 105MG; CARBOHYDRATES 1G; SUGAR 0G; FIBER 0G; PROTEIN 0G

Cool as a Cucumber-Avocado Soup

This cool cucumber refresher is the perfect stress reducer.

Ingredients

2 ripe avocados, pitted and peeled

½ yellow pepper, seeded, cut in 1-inch chunks

1 jalapeño, seeded

½ cup packed fresh cilantro leaves

2 cloves garlic

1½ teaspoons salt

2 tablespoons freshly squeezed lemon juice

2¼ cups low-sodium chicken broth

8-inch piece English cucumber, cut into 2-inch chunks

Directions

1 Place all ingredients into the XL Capacity 48-ounce Nutri Ninja® in the order listed.

2 Select Auto-iQ™ XL EXTRACTION.

3 Chill before serving.

NUTRITIONALS (PER SERVING): CALORIES 190; FAT 14G; SODIUM 50MG; CARBOHYDRATES 15G; SUGAR 2G; FIBER 7G; PROTEIN 5G

PREP TIME: 15 minutes   COOK TIME: 30 minutes   SERVINGS: 4   CONTAINER: XL Capacity 48-ounce Nutri Ninja®

Curried Carrot Soup

This delicious beta-carotene-rich carrot soup is fantastic with the added Indian flavor.

Ingredients

2 teaspoons extra-virgin olive oil

3 garlic cloves

1 small yellow onion, quartered

¼ teaspoon salt

¼ teaspoon ground black pepper

2 teaspoons red curry paste

2¼ cups peeled carrots, cut in 1-inch chunks

2¼ cups low-sodium chicken broth

1¼ cups light coconut milk

Directions

1 Preheat a 3-quart saucepan over medium heat. Add the oil and sauté the garlic and onions for 3 to 5 minutes, stirring until translucent.

2 Add the salt, black pepper, red curry paste, carrots, and chicken broth to the saucepan. Bring to a boil, reduce the heat to medium-low, and cook for 20 to 25 minutes or until the carrots are fork tender.

3 Remove from heat, add the coconut milk and cool to room temperature.

4 Place half of the cooled soup into the XL Capacity 48-ounce Nutri Ninja®.

5 Select Auto-iQ™ XL EXTRACTION. Return puréed soup to saucepan and simmer until heated through.

NUTRITIONALS (PER SERVING): CALORIES 60; FAT 3G; SODIUM 320MG; CARBOHYDRATES 7G; SUGAR 7G; FIBER 2G; PROTEIN 2G

Kale & Celery Root Soup

Here's a new twist on traditional pesto. It's a great way to use up extra greens.

Ingredients

1 tablespoon olive oil

3 cloves garlic

1 small yellow onion, quartered

¾ cup chopped celery root

¾ cup packed kale leaves

1½ teaspoons salt

¾ teaspoon ground black pepper

4½ cups low-sodium vegetable broth

Directions

1 Preheat a 5-quart saucepan over medium heat.

2 Add the oil, garlic, and onions. Gently stir to sauté for 3 to 5 minutes or until translucent.

3 Add the remaining ingredients, bring to a boil, reduce heat to medium-low, and simmer for 20 to 25 minutes or until the celery root is fork tender.

4 Remove from heat and cool to room temperature.

5 Place the cooled soup into the XL Capacity 48-ounce Nutri Ninja®.

6 Select Auto-iQ™ XL EXTRACTION. Return puréed soup to saucepan and simmer until heated through.

NUTRITIONALS (PER SERVING): CALORIES 60; FAT 2.5G; SODIUM 1370MG; CARBOHYDRATES 11G; SUGAR 3G; FIBER 1G; PROTEIN 1G

Chilled Spanish Tomato Soup

This soup is simple and refreshing in the height of summer, when tomatoes are ripest. Serve with chopped hard boiled eggs, crispy Serrano ham, and a drizzle of some delicious olive oil.

Ingredients

2-inch thick piece of baguette, quartered

1 cup warm water

3 vine-ripe tomatoes, cored, quartered

1 clove garlic

⅛ cup dry-roasted almonds

¼ cup olive oil

¾ teaspoon sherry vinegar

¾ teaspoon salt

⅛ teaspoon ground black pepper

Directions

1 Place the baguette and warm water into a small bowl and let sit for 10 minutes, allowing the bread to soften. In a mesh strainer set over a medium bowl, squeeze out the tomato seeds from each quartered piece. Set the quartered, cleaned tomatoes aside. Push the seeds around in the mesh strainer to release as much liquid as possible. Reserve the extracted liquid and discard the remaining seeds.

2 Squeeze the baguette of excess liquid and place baguette into the Regular 24-ounce Nutri Ninja® Cup or the Stainless Steel Nutri Ninja®. Add the tomatoes, tomato liquid, garlic, almonds, olive oil, sherry vinegar, salt, and pepper.

3 Select Auto-iQ™ PRO EXTRACTION.

4 Chill at least 2 hours before serving. Adjust seasonings and garnish with your desired toppings!

NUTRITIONALS (PER SERVING): CALORIES 370; FAT 32G; SODIUM 840MG; CARBOHYDRATES 20G; SUGAR 5G; FIBER 4G; PROTEIN 6G

Pot 'O Gold Cauliflower Soup

This healthy, vegan soup is packed with flavor and is as satisfying as a main course.

Ingredients

1 tablespoon coconut oil

1 yellow onion, quartered

3 cups cauliflower florets

4½ cups low-sodium vegetable broth

1 teaspoon ground turmeric

¾ teaspoon ground cumin

½ teaspoon ground mustard

½ teaspoon cayenne

salt and pepper to taste

1 lime cut into wedges

2 tablespoons chopped cilantro

Directions

1 Heat coconut oil in a medium-size saucepan over medium heat and sauté the onions for 3 to 5 minutes, until softened. Add cauliflower to saucepan and sauté for 5 minutes.

2 Add vegetable broth, turmeric, cumin, ground mustard, and cayenne. Set stove to high and bring to a boil. Turn heat to low and simmer, covered for 20 to 25 minutes or until cauliflower is softened. Let cool to room temperature.

3 Place cooled soup into the XL Capacity 48-ounce Nutri Ninja® and select Auto-iQ™ XL EXTRACTION.

4 Return soup to the saucepan, and simmer until heated through. Season to taste with salt and pepper.

5 To serve, squeeze lime juice on top of soup in individual bowls and sprinkle with cilantro.

NUTRITIONALS (PER SERVING): CALORIES 100; FAT 4.5G; SODIUM 540MG; CARBOHYDRATES 12G; SUGAR 6G; FIBER 3G; PROTEIN 3G

SAUCES/SOUPS/ENTRÉES

Black Bean Soup

Slightly spicy and very creamy, this luscious soup warms you to the bone.

Ingredients

1 teaspoon olive oil

½ small yellow onion, quartered

1 carrot, peeled and chopped

1 stalk celery, trimmed and chopped

2 cloves garlic, chopped

2 teaspoons ground cumin

1 teaspoon dried oregano

3 cups cooked black beans, drained

2 chipotle peppers

1¾ cups low-sodium chicken broth

¼ teaspoon salt

Sliced ripe avocado

Mexican or Jack cheese, crumbled

Directions

1 Heat oil in a 3-quart saucepan on medium-high heat and sauté onion, carrot, celery, garlic, cumin, and oregano until vegetables are softened. Cool to room temperature.

2 Place the cooled vegetables, black beans, chipotle peppers, chicken broth, salt, and pepper into the XL Capacity 48-ounce Nutri Ninja®.

3 Select Auto-iQ™ XL EXTRACTION.

4 Return puréed soup to saucepan and simmer until heated through.

5 Serve each with avocado and cheese.

NUTRITIONALS (PER SERVING): CALORIES 129;
FAT 1G; CHOLESTEROL 0MG;
SODIUM 690MG; CARBOHYDRATE 30G;
FIBER 8G; PROTEIN 8G

Almond-Dijon Baked Fish

Use this delicious crunchy herb topping with your favorite white fish, cod, haddock, and more.

Ingredients

1 cup whole almonds

½ cup fresh parsley leaves

⅛ teaspoon salt

⅛ teaspoon ground black pepper

½ cup Dijon mustard

4 fillets (4 ounces each) favorite white fish

Directions

1 Preheat oven to 400°F. Place the fish fillets onto a foil-lined sheet tray and evenly brush with Dijon. Set aside.

2 Place almonds, parsley, salt, and pepper into the Stainless Steel Nutri Ninja® in the order listed.

3 PULSE 3 to 5 times, using long pulses.

4 Evenly top the fish fillets with the almond coating. Bake for 10 to 15 minutes until fish flakes easily with a fork.

NUTRITIONALS (PER SERVING): CALORIES 320; FAT 20G; SODIUM 200MG; CARBOHYDRATES 9G; SUGAR 1G; FIBER 5G; PROTEIN 31G

PREP TIME: 10 minutes   COOK TIME: 20–25 minutes   SERVINGS: 4   CONTAINER: Stainless Steel Nutri Ninja®

Corn Flake-Crusted Thyme Chicken Breasts

This will become your favorite crunchy chicken recipe. Thyme and chicken are made to go together.

Ingredients

3 cups of corn flakes

1 tablespoon fresh thyme leaves or
   1½ tablespoons dried thyme leaves

2 teaspoon salt

½ teaspoon pepper

1 cup low-fat buttermilk

4 boneless skinless chicken breasts

Directions

1 Preheat oven to 350°F. Place corn flakes, thyme, salt, and pepper into the Stainless Steel Nutri Ninja®.

2 PULSE 3 to 5 times, using long pulses. Pour into medium baking dish; set aside.

3 Pour buttermilk into shallow dish and dip chicken breasts in buttermilk.

4 Roll chicken breasts in corn flake mixture. Place coated chicken breasts onto a non-stick sheet tray. Lightly spray breaded chicken with olive oil.

5 Bake 20 to 25 minutes, gently flipping chicken breasts halfway through until golden brown and chicken is cooked through.

NUTRITIONALS (PER SERVING) CALORIES 300; FAT 5G; SODIUM 880MG; CARBOHYDRATES 22G; SUGAR 5G; FIBER 1G; PROTEIN 39G;

PREP TIME: 15 minutes   COOK TIME: 10–15 minutes   SERVINGS: 4   CONTAINER: Stainless Steel Nutri Ninja®

Coconut-Macadamia Encrusted Shrimp

This delicious homemade crust also tastes great with Halibut and Mahi-mahi.

Ingredients

½ cup unsweetened coconut flakes

½ cup macadamia nuts

4 slices of dry stale or lightly toasted bread, torn into small pieces

¼ teaspoon salt

1 egg

¾ cup coconut milk

2 cups all-purpose flour

1 pound peeled, deveined shrimp (16/20 ct.)

4 tablespoons honey

1 tablespoon Dijon mustard

Directions

1 Preheat oven to 425°F. Place a roasting rack on a sheet tray and set aside.

2 Place coconut flakes, macadamia nuts, bread, and salt into the Stainless Steel Nutri Ninja® in the order listed.

3 PULSE 5 to 7 times, using long pulses. Pour into a medium dish; set aside.

4 In medium mixing bowl, beat egg and milk together; set aside. Lightly dust shrimp with the flour, then immerse into the egg/milk mixture, and roll in the macadamia coating.

5 Place the coated shrimp on the roasting rack. Lightly spray the shrimp with olive oil.

6 Bake 10 to 15 minutes or until golden brown. While baking, combine the honey and Dijon mustard in a small bowl. Serve immediately.

NUTRITIONALS (PER SERVING): CALORIES 360; FAT 19G; SODIUM 530MG; CARBOHYDRATES 41G; SUGAR 19G; FIBER 3G; PROTEIN 11G

PREP TIME: 15 minutes   COOK TIME: 10–15 minutes   SERVINGS: 4   CONTAINER: Stainless Steel Nutri Ninja®

Crispy Parmesan Zucchini Fries

This delicious homemade Parmesan coating also works great with chicken and white fish.

Ingredients

2 large zucchini

6 slices dried stale or lightly toasted bread

½ cup fresh parsley leaves

3-ounce chunk Parmesan cheese cut into 4 pieces

½ teaspoon garlic powder

½ teaspoon red chili flakes

¼ teaspoon salt

1 egg

¾ cup milk

2 cups all-purpose flour

Olive oil spray

Sundried Tomato Sauce, page 54, warmed

Directions

1 Preheat oven to 425°F. Place a roasting rack onto a sheet tray and lightly spray with olive oil; set aside. To cut the zucchini, halve each widthwise so you have 4 cylinders. Cut each cylinder in half lengthwise then cut each of those halves into 4 wedges. You will have 32 wedges; set aside.

2 Place bread, parsley, Parmesan cheese, garlic powder, chili flakes, and salt into the Stainless Steel Nutri Ninja® in the order listed. PULSE 5 to 7 times, using long pulses. Pour into a deep baking dish. Set aside.

3 In medium mixing bowl, beat egg and milk together; set aside. Lightly dust zucchini wedges with the flour. Immerse zucchini wedges into egg/milk mixture, coating thoroughly, then roll zucchini into the Parmesan mixture.

4 Place coated zucchini wedges onto the roasting rack and lightly spray zucchini with olive oil. Bake for 10–15 minutes until golden brown. Serve immediately with the tomato sauce.

NUTRITIONALS (PER SERVING): CALORIES 280; FAT 8G; SODIUM 510MG; CARBOHYDRATES 40G; SUGAR 8G; FIBER 3G; PROTEIN 12G

Muhammara
page 71

Frozen White Russian

Normally a creamy, decadent treat, this frozen favorite is lightened up with almond milk.

Ingredients

3½ cups ice

¼ cup vodka

¼ cup + 2 tablespoons coffee liqueur

1 tablespoon instant espresso powder

1¼ cups unsweetened almond milk

Directions

1 Place all ingredients into the XL Capacity 48-ounce Nutri Ninja® in the order listed.

2 Select Auto-iQ™ XL EXTRACTION.

NUTRITIONALS (PER SERVING): CALORIES 130; FAT 1G; SODIUM 65MG; CARBOHYDRATES 10G; SUGAR 8G; FIBER 0G; PROTEIN 0G

NINJA KNOW-HOW   USE ANY OTHER NON-DAIRY MILK TO KEEP THIS COCKTAIL VEGAN-FRIENDLY.

Pear-Ginger Sake Martini

Spicy and sweet flavors explode in this exotic cocktail.

Ingredients

1 large ripe pear

¼-inch piece fresh peeled ginger

2 cups pear juice

¾ cup sake

1 tablespoon agave nectar

1 cup ice

Directions

1 Peel, core, and quarter the pear. Place on a parchment-line sheet tray. Freeze until firm.

2 Place all ingredients into the XL Capacity 48-ounce Nutri Ninja® in the order listed.

3 Select Auto-iQ™ XL EXTRACTION.

4 Serve in martini glasses.

NUTRITIONALS (PER SERVING): CALORIES 156; FAT 0G; SODIUM 14MG; CARBOHYDRATE 27G; SUGAR 4G; FIBER 1G; PROTEIN 0G

ENTERTAINING

Fresh Citrus Margarita

Using citrus fruit makes this classic drink taste fresher and controls the calories!

Ingredients

4 cups ice

1 lime, peeled, cut in half

½ lemon, peeled

¾ cup orange juice

¼ cup triple sec

⅔ cup silver tequila

2 teaspoons agave nectar

Directions

1 Place all ingredients into the XL Capacity 48-ounce Nutri Ninja® in the order listed.

2 Select Auto-iQ™ XL EXTRACTION.

NUTRITIONALS (PER SERVING): CALORIES 190; FAT 0G; SODIUM 5MG; CARBOHYDRATES 17G; SUGAR 13G; FIBER 1G; PROTEIN 1G

Frozen Peach Bellini

This refreshing take on the Italian classic makes an impressive cocktail.

Ingredients

2½ cups frozen peach slices

1 cup ice

¼ cup peach schnapps

1 tablespoon superfine sugar

1½ teaspoons lemon juice

3 cups chilled Prosecco

Directions

1 Place all ingredients into the XL Capacity 48-ounce Nutri Ninja® in the order listed.

2 Select Auto-iQ™ XL EXTRACTION.

NUTRITIONALS (PER SERVING): CALORIES 230; FAT 0G; SODIUM 0MG; CARBOHYDRATES 26G; SUGAR 14G; FIBER 1G; PROTEIN 1G

Curry Bloody Mary

Using fresh vegetables and exotic spices makes this a delicious choice versus store mixes.

Ingredients

2 small celery stalks, quartered, plus extra stalk for garnish

1 lemon, peeled, seeded

4 small vine-ripe tomatoes, quartered

1 cup carrot juice

2 teaspoons green curry paste

1 teaspoon tamarind concentrate

4 dashes hot sauce

Small pinch celery seed

½ cup vodka

4 cups ice

Directions

1 Place all ingredients, except the ice, into the XL Capacity 48-ounce Nutri Ninja® in the order listed.

2 Select Auto-iQ™ XL EXTRACTION.

3 Serve over ice and garnish with a celery stalk.

NUTRITIONALS (PER SERVING): CALORIES 120; FAT 1G; SODIUM 35MG; CARBOHYDRATES 12G; SUGAR 6G; FIBER 2G; PROTEIN 2G

NINJA KNOW-HOW SERVE WITHOUT ALCOHOL FOR A NUTRIENT EXTRACT JUICE FILLED WITH ANTIOXIDANTS.

Muhammara

Just the right amounts of heat, sweet, and spice make this Middle Eastern dip perfect for serving with lightly toasted pita triangles or crudité.

Ingredients

1 jar (7 ounces) roasted red peppers, drained, ½ cup liquid reserved

¼ of an 8-inch round pita, torn into small pieces

1 cup toasted walnut pieces

2 tablespoons lemon juice

2 tablespoons tomato paste

1 tablespoon Aleppo pepper

1 tablespoon sumac

1 tablespoon Harissa paste

1½ teaspoons pomegranate molasses

1 teaspoon ground cumin

2 tablespoons olive oil

salt and pepper to taste

Directions

1 Soak pita in the ½ cup of liquid from the roasted peppers until soft (2 to 3 minutes). Remove pita and discard additional liquid.

2 Place pita and remaining ingredients, into the Regular 24-ounce Nutri Ninja® Cup or the Stainless Steel Nutri Ninja® in the order listed.

3 Select Auto-iQ™ PRO EXTRACTION.

NUTRITIONALS (PER 2 TABLESPOON SERVING): CALORIES 90; FAT 8G; SODIUM 140MG; CARBOHYDRATES 5G; SUGAR 2G; FIBER 1G; PROTEIN 2G;

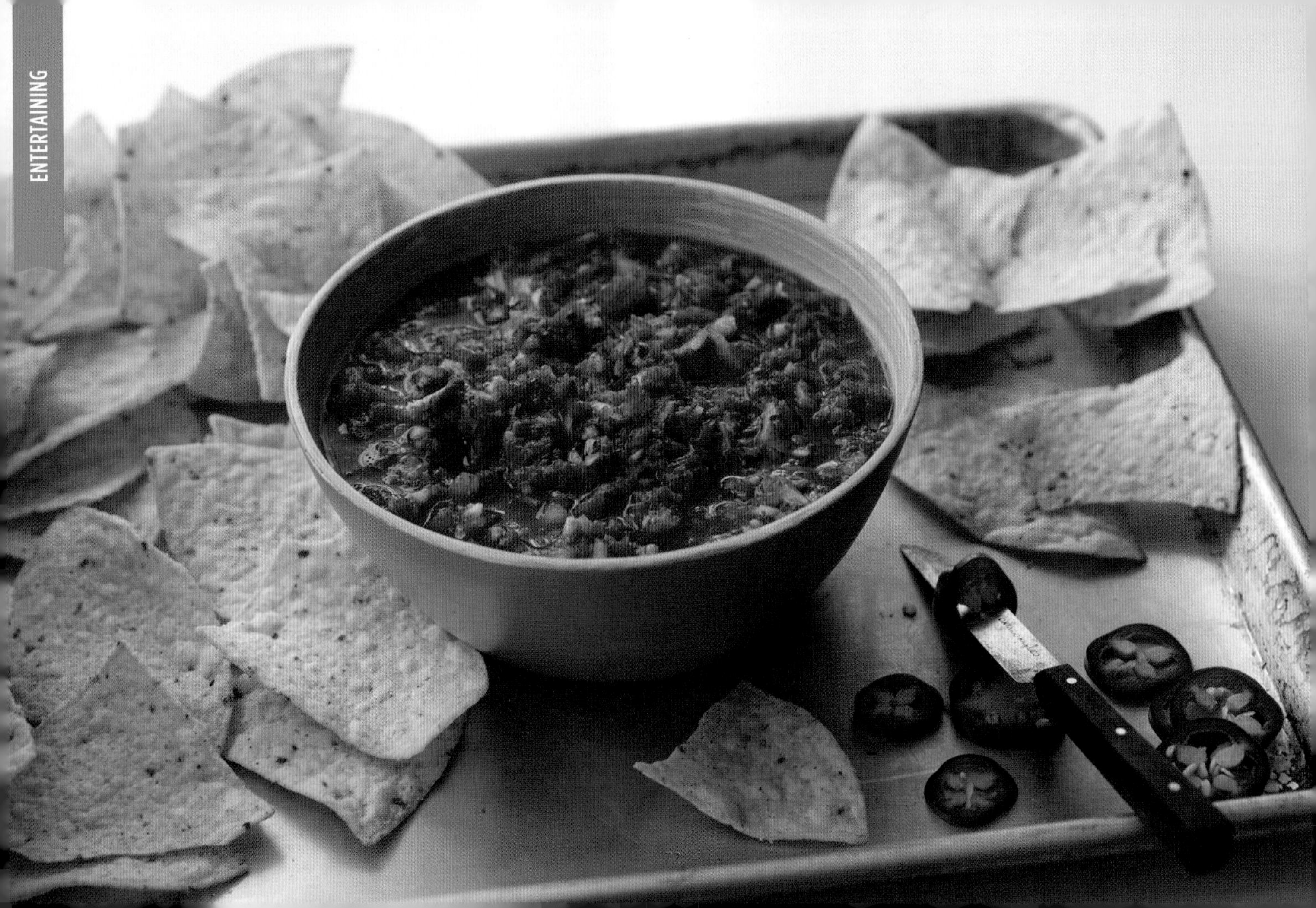

PREP TIME: 4 minutes   MAKES: 2 cups   CONTAINER: Regular 24-ounce Nutri Ninja® Cup/Stainless Steel Nutri Ninja®

Best Blender Salsa

You can depend on the flavor of this salsa every time! Canned tomatoes create consistency and rich flavor.

Ingredients

1 can (14 ounces) whole peeled tomatoes

½ white onion, quartered

½ jalapeño, seeds removed

½ chipotle chili, in adobo

1 tablespoon adobo sauce

½ lime, peeled, quartered

¼ teaspoon salt

⅛ teaspoon ground black pepper

Directions

1 Place all ingredients into the Regular 24-ounce Nutri Ninja® Cup or the Stainless Steel Nutri Ninja® in the order listed.

2 PULSE 3 to 5 times, to desired consistency.

NUTRITIONALS (PER 1/2 CUP SERVING): CALORIES 30; FAT 0G; SODIUM 220G; CARBOHYDRATES 7G; SUGAR 3G; FIBER 2G; PROTEIN 1G

FOR A TROPICAL VARIATION, ADD ½ CUP FRESH MANGO TO THE NUTRI® NINJA CUP BEFORE PULSING.

PREP TIME: 25 min. + 9 min. cooking   MAKES: 1½ cups   CONTAINER: Regular 24-ounce Nutri Ninja® Cup/Stainless Steel Nutri Ninja®

French Onion Tofu Dip

A healthier option without all the added fat; so delicious!

Ingredients

1 tablespoon vegetable oil

1 medium yellow onion, chopped

½ teaspoon salt

¼ teaspoon ground black pepper

3 tablespoons malt vinegar

½ cup firm tofu

½ cup nonfat cream cheese, softened

⅓ cup nonfat sour cream

Directions

1 In a 10-inch sauté pan at medium heat, add the oil, onion, salt, and black pepper. Cook 6 to 8 minutes or until caramelized, stirring occasionally. Add the malt vinegar and cook for 1 minute.

2 Remove from the heat and let cool for 10 minutes.

3 Place the cooked onion mixture, tofu, cream cheese, and sour cream into the Regular 24-ounce Nutri Ninja® Cup or the Stainless Steel Nutri Ninja®.

4 PULSE 3 times, using short pulses, then select START and then blend for 15 seconds.

NUTRITIONALS (PER 1/2 CUP SERVING): CALORIES 150; FAT 7G; SODIUM 650MG; CARBOHYDRATES 12G; SUGAR 6G; FIBER 1G; PROTEIN 11G

PREP TIME: 15 minutes   COOK TIME: 20-25 minutes   MAKES: 4 cups   CONTAINER: Stainless Steel Nutri Ninja®/XL Capacity 48-ounce Nutri Ninja®

ENTERTAINING

Roasted Eggplant Za'atar Dip

This homemade Za'atar dip can be served with crudité, pita chips, or vegetable crisps.

Ingredients

1 large eggplant, peeled and cut into ½-inch slices

2 tablespoons olive oil

2 tablespoons dried oregano leaves

2 tablespoons sumac

2 tablespoons toasted, unsalted sesame seeds

2 tablespoon dried marjoram leaves

½ teaspoon red pepper flakes

1 teaspoon salt

1 teaspoon ground black pepper

1½ cups plain Greek yogurt

2 tablespoon lemon juice

Directions

1 Preheat oven to 500°F. Place eggplant slices in a single layer on a lightly oiled baking sheet. Brush each slice with the olive oil. Bake 20 to 25 minutes; set aside.

2 Place oregano, sumac, marjoram, sesame, red pepper flakes, salt, and pepper into the Stainless Steel Nutri Ninja® in the order listed. PULSE 5 to 7 times, using long pulses.

3 Place the yogurt, lemon juice, cooled eggplant, and 3 tablespoons of the Za'atar mixture into the XL Capacity 48-ounce Nutri Ninja®. Select Auto-iQ™ XL EXTRACTION.

4 PULSE longer for a smoother texture. Serve the dip with a pinch of additional Za'atar seasoning on top.

NUTRITIONALS (PER SERVING): CALORIES 120; FAT 7G; SODIUM 420MG; CARBOHYDRATES 9G; SUGAR 4G; FIBER 4G; PROTEIN 8G

Smokey Black Bean Dip

Chipotle peppers add a subtle smoky heat to this delicious dip that is sure to be a crowd pleaser!

Ingredients

½ cup cubed Cheddar cheese, about 3 ounces

1 can (15.5 ounces) low-sodium black beans

2 chipotle peppers in adobo

1 tablespoon adobo sauce

1 clove garlic

½ teaspoon ground cumin

¼ teaspoon salt

¼ cup loosely packed cilantro leaves

1 tablespoon lime juice

⅓ cup water

Directions

1 Preheat oven to 350°F. Place all ingredients into the Regular 24-ounce Nutri Ninja® Cup or the Stainless Steel Nutri Ninja® in the order listed.

2 PULSE 3 times, using short pulses, then select START and blend for 30 seconds.

3 Place into an oven-proof dish and bake 5 to 7 minutes, until warmed through. Serve with tortilla chips.

NUTRITIONALS (PER ½ CUP SERVING): CALORIES 100; FAT 4G; SODIUM 590MG; CARBOHYDRATES 10G; SUGAR 2G; FIBER 3G; PROTEIN 6G

Lemon Tart with
Pistachio Crust
page 87

PREP TIME: 4 minutes   SERVINGS: 12   CONTAINER: Stainless Steel Nutri Ninja®

Chocolate Walnut Dessert Topping

This topping is excellent on ice cream, but also tastes great with French toast, pancakes, and waffles.

Ingredients

2 ounces 70% cacao extra-bitter chocolate, chopped

1 cup walnut pieces

½ teaspoon ground cinnamon

2 tablespoons light brown sugar

Directions

1 Place all ingredients into the Stainless Steel Nutri Ninja® in the order listed.

2 PULSE 5 to 7 times, using long pulses. Store in airtight container in refrigerator.

NUTRITIONALS (PER 2 TABLESPOON SERVING): CALORIES 120; FAT 11G; SODIUM 0MG; CARBOHYDRATES 6G; SUGAR 3G; FIBER 1G; PROTEIN 2G

Frozen Hot Chocolate

Everyone's favorite winter beverage, blended into a cool, thick treat to enjoy with friends.

Ingredients

2 cups low-fat milk, separated

½ cup instant nonfat dry milk

5 tablespoons unsweetened cocoa powder

4 tablespoons agave nectar

Pinch salt

3 cups ice

Directions

1 In a bowl, combine 1 cup of the milk with the instant nonfat dry milk, cocoa powder, agave, and salt. Stir with a whisk or a fork until all ingredients have formed a smooth slurry.

2 Add the ice to the XL 48-ounce Capacity Nutri Ninja® followed by the slurry and the last cup of milk.

3 Select Auto-iQ™ XL EXTRACTION.

NUTRITIONALS (PER SERVING): CALORIES 160; FAT 2G; SODIUM 180MG; CARBOHYDRATES 31G; SUGAR 27G; FIBER 2G; PROTEIN 9G

Honey-Nut Frozen Treat

Here's a honey of a frozen dessert that whips up in minutes. Spoon into dessert dishes and serve with a drizzle of honey. Double delicious!

Ingredients

2 cups original oat milk

1 cup walnut pieces

½ teaspoon vanilla extract

3 cups ice

3 tablespoons honey

Directions

1 Place all ingredients into the XL Capacity 48-ounce Nutri Ninja® in the order listed.

2 Select Auto-iQ™ XL EXTRACTION.

NUTRITIONALS (PER SERVING): CALORIES 280; FAT 18G; SODIUM 60MG; CARBOHYDRATES 28G; SUGAR 22G; FIBER 3G; PROTEIN 6G

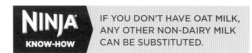

NINJA® KNOW-HOW IF YOU DON'T HAVE OAT MILK, ANY OTHER NON-DAIRY MILK CAN BE SUBSTITUTED.

Mango Cream

This is a really delicious recipe for a homemade yogurt treat without all the calories of the commercial stuff.

Ingredients

3 cups frozen mango chunks

1 cup nonfat yogurt

3 tablespoons honey

1½ cups coconut water

Directions

1 Place all ingredients into the XL Capacity 48-ounce Nutri Ninja® in the order listed.

2 Select Auto-iQ™ XL EXTRACTION.

NUTRITIONALS (PER SERVING): CALORIES 170; FAT .5G; SODIUM 120MG; CARBOHYDRATES 37G; SUGAR 35G; FIBER 3G; PROTEIN 8G

PREP TIME: 15 minutes   SERVINGS: 4   CONTAINER: Regular 24-ounce Nutri Ninja® Cup/Stainless Steel Nutri Ninja®

Banana Chocolate Mousse

Avocado is the secret ingredient in this decadent dessert.

Ingredients

2 small ripe bananas, cut in quarters

2 ripe avocados, pitted, peeled, and quartered

¼ cup chocolate syrup

½ orange, juiced

¼ cup cocoa powder

Directions

1 Place all ingredients into the Regular 24-ounce Nutri Ninja® Cup or the Stainless Steel Nutri Ninja® in the order listed.

2 Select Auto-iQ™ PRO EXTRACTION.

NUTRITIONALS (PER SERVING): CALORIES 280; FAT 16G; SODIUM 25MG; CARBOHYDRATES 39G; SUGAR 19G; FIBER 11G; PROTEIN 4G

NINJA KNOW-HOW   REPLACE THE CHOCOLATE SYRUP WITH 2 OUNCES OF MELTED DARK CHOCOLATE IN THE MICROWAVE FOR A RICHER FLAVOR.

Monkey Madness

A healthier version than the chunky chocolate-banana treat.

Ingredients

1 small ripe banana, cut in half

2 tablespoons unsweetened cocoa powder

1¼ cups almond milk

1 tablespoon agave nectar

¼ cup almond butter

1 cup ice

Directions

1 Place all ingredients into the Regular 24-ounce Nutri Ninja® Cup or the Stainless Steel Nutri Ninja® in the order listed.

2 Select Auto-iQ™ PRO EXTRACTION.

NUTRITIONALS (PER SERVING): CALORIES 230; FAT 13G; SODIUM 65MG; CARBOHYDRATES 27G; SUGAR 17G; FIBER 5G; PROTEIN 6G

NINJA® KNOW-HOW ADD 2 TABLESPOONS CACAO NIBS FOR A SUPER FOOD BOOST!

SWEET TREATS

Hazelnut-Topped Apple Crisp

For all seasons, this homemade Hazelnut topping is great with your favorite fruit crisp. Try it with the seasons best—pears, strawberries, or even plums!

Ingredients

FOR THE FILLING:

2 tablespoons butter, softened to room temperature

2 large Granny Smith apples, peeled, cored, and diced

½ cup pitted prunes, chopped

⅓ cup sugar

3 tablespoons packed golden brown sugar

2 teaspoons all-purpose flour

2 teaspoons ground cinnamon

FOR THE TOPPING:

⅓ cup packed brown sugar

1 teaspoon cinnamon

¼ cup all-purpose flour

¼ cup old-fashioned rolled oats

1 cup hazelnuts

¼ teaspoon salt

¼ cup unsalted butter softened to room temperature

Directions

1 Preheat oven to 375°F. Butter 8-inch glass baking dish; set aside.

2 In a large bowl combine apples, prunes, both sugars, flour, and cinnamon. Mix well then place into the buttered baking dish. Bake until edges begin to bubble, about 20 minutes.

3 While baking, prepare topping by placing sugar, cinnamon, flour, oatmeal, hazelnuts and salt into the Stainless Steel Nutri Ninja®. PULSE 5 to 7 times, using long pulses.

4 Pour mixture into a medium-mixing bowl and add butter, using fingertips to rub it into mixture until clumps form.

5 Scatter topping over fruit filling. Continue baking until topping is a golden and juices are bubbling thick, about 20 minutes.

NUTRITIONALS: 1 SERVING: CALORIES 370; FAT 20G; SODIUM 140MG; CARBOHYDRATES 50G; SUGAR 28G; FIBER 4G; PROTEIN 4G

Apple Pie Smoothie

The classic flavors of apple pie transformed into a creamy, smooth drink to serve morning anytime, morning 'til night.

Ingredients

2 large Golden Delicious apples, peeled, cored and each cut into eighths

1 tablespoon packed brown sugar

½ teaspoon ground cinnamon

⅛ teaspoon ground nutmeg

¼ teaspoon salt

1½ teaspoons lemon juice

2 cups unsweetened almond milk

2 cups ice

Directions

1 Place all ingredients into the XL Capacity 48-ounce Nutri Ninja® in the order listed.

2 Select Auto-iQ™ XL EXTRACTION.

NUTRITIONALS (PER SERVING): CALORIES 80; FAT 1.5G; SODIUM 240MG; CARBOHYDRATES 18G; SUGAR 14G; FIBER 2G; PROTEIN 1G

SWEET TREATS

Tropical Fresh Fruit Ice Pops

Mango and pineapple make this a tropical treat. With the addition of agave nectar, it is still only 80 calories per pop.

Ingredients

1 cup fresh mango chunks

2 cups fresh pineapple chunks

2 tablespoons agave nectar

Directions

1 Place all ingredients into the Regular 24-ounce Nutri Ninja® Cup or the Stainless SteelNutri Ninja® in the order listed.

2 Select Auto-iQ™ PRO EXTRACTION.

3 Pour into preferred shape frozen treat molds and freeze overnight or until solid.

NUTRITIONALS (PER POPSICLE): CALORIES 60; FAT 0G; SODIUM 0MG; CARBOHYDRATES 15G; SUGAR 13G; FIBER 1G; PROTEIN 1G

Lemon Tart with Pistachio Crust

The pistachios lend a unique nuttiness to the bright citrus flavor that comes from using the lemon peel. Your taste buds will be delighted!

Ingredients

PISTACHIO CRUST:

1 cup whole raw pistachios

½ cup all-purpose flour

¼ cup sugar

¼ teaspoon salt

¼ cup butter, melted

½ teaspoon vanilla extract

LEMON CURD:

1 organic lemon, washed, quartered and seeds removed

1 cup sugar

3 tablespoons lemon juice

3 large eggs

¼ cup butter, melted

Directions

1 Preheat oven to 350°F. Place the pistachios into the Stainless Steel Nutri Ninja® and PULSE, using long pulses, until finely ground. Place pistachio flour into a medium bowl and add all-purpose flour, sugar, salt, melted butter, and vanilla extract. Stir with a fork until fully incorporated. Lightly coat a 8-inch tart pan with nonstick cooking spray and press crust mixture into pan. Bake 13 to 15 minutes or until lightly golden brown.

2 Reduce heat to 300°F. Place lemon, sugar, lemon juice, eggs, and melted butter into a clean Stainless Steel Nutri Ninja®.

3 Select Auto-iQ™ PRO EXTRACTION.

4 Pour lemon mixture into crust and bake for 20 minutes or until just set in center. Let cool. Store in refrigerator.

NUTRITIONALS (PER SERVING): CALORIES 250; FAT 14G; SODIUM 135MG; CARBOHYDRATES 29G SUGAR 22G; FIBER 1G; PROTEIN 4G

Index